P9-BYY-818

This book belongs to:
Noblesville East Middle School
300 N. 17th Street
Noblesville, IN 46060

WITHDRAWN

THE 10™

Greatest Breakthroughs in Space Exploration

Julie Clark

Series Editor
Jeffrey D. Wilhelm

Much thought, debate, and research went into choosing and ranking the 10 items in each book in this series. We realize that everyone has his or her own opinion of what is most significant, revolutionary, amazing, deadly, and so on. As you read, you may agree with our choices, or you may be surprised — and that's the way it should be!

an imprint of

◼ SCHOLASTIC

www.scholastic.com/librarypublishing

A Rubicon book published in association with Scholastic Inc.

Rubicon © 2008 Rubicon Publishing Inc.
www.rubiconpublishing.com

All rights reserved. No part of this publication may be reproduced, stored in a database or retrieval system, distributed, or transmitted in any form or by any means, electronic, mechanical, photocopying, recording, or otherwise, without the prior written permission of Rubicon Publishing Inc.

 is a trademark of The 10 Books

SCHOLASTIC and associated logos and designs are trademarks and/or registered trademarks of Scholastic Inc.

Associate Publishers: Kim Koh, Miriam Bardswich
Project Editor: Amy Land
Editor: Bettina Fehrenbach
Creative Director: Jennifer Drew
Project Manager/Designer: Jeanette MacLean
Graphic Designers: Waseem Bashar, Brandon Köpke

The publisher gratefully acknowledges the following for permission to reprint copyrighted material in this book.

Every reasonable effort has been made to trace the owners of copyrighted material and to make due acknowledgment. Any errors or omissions drawn to our attention will be gladly rectified in future editions.

"The Lost Rover" (excerpt) from "Mars probe may have spotted lost rover" by Maggie McKee. From NewScientist.com, January 12, 2007. Reprinted with permission from *New Scientist* magazine.

"Canada and the International Space Station" (excerpt). From CBC News, January 15, 2006. Permission courtesy of CBC.ca.

"Surviving space and fame" (excerpt) by Olga Sobolevskaya. From *The Hindu*, April 16, 2006. Copyright *The Hindu* 2006. Permission for publication is approved.

Cover: Astronaut–NASA

Library and Archives Canada Cataloguing in Publication

Clark, Julie
    The 10 greatest breakthroughs in space exploration / Julie Clark.

Includes index.
ISBN 978-1-55448-520-8

    1. Readers (Elementary). 2. Readers—Space flights. I. Title.
II. Title: Ten most breakthroughs in space exploration.

PE1117.C56 2007a   428.6   C2007-906690-9

1 2 3 4 5 6 7 8 9 10   10   17 16 15 14 13 12 11 10 09 08

Printed in Singapore

32222000182578

Contents

BLAST-OFF!

Do you ever look up at the sky and wonder what is up there? Are there planets that haven't been discovered? Are there other life-forms on other planets? This curiosity has led to some of the most significant breakthroughs in space exploration.

The earliest space explorers studied the universe from Earth. They used only their eyes and telescopes. The invention of rockets and satellites in the early 20th century boosted scientific understanding of outer space. By the mid-20th century, space exploration involving human beings became a reality. It turned into a space race between the former Soviet Union and the United States. Many extraordinary space missions took place, one after the other.

In this book, we present what we think are the 10 greatest breakthroughs in space exploration. In ranking them, we did not follow the order in which the breakthroughs took place. Instead we considered these criteria: the breakthrough mission or equipment opened new frontiers; it successfully used new technology; it advanced scientific discoveries; it added to existing knowledge about space and the solar system; it created friendly ties between countries; and it led to memorable space missions.

SPACE SHUTTLE–NASA

SPACE TIMELINE

- 1957: *Sputnik* Satellites

- 1962: *Vostok 1*

- 1962: Planetary Space Probes

WHAT IS THE GREATEST BREAKTHROUGH IN SPACE EXPLORATION?

- 1969: *Apollo 11*
- 1981: *Columbia* Space Shuttle
- 1981: Canadarm
- 1986: Mir Space Station

- 1990: Hubble Space Telescope
- 1996: *Sojourner* Rover
- 1998: International Space Station

(10) INTERNATIONAL

In order to complete the International Space Station, astronauts will spend 1,900 hours to assemble over one million pounds of hardware.

ISS–NASA

SPACE STATION

LAUNCH DATE: November 20, 1998 — with the first section

LENGTH OF MISSION: Ongoing and will last many years into the future

BLAZING THE TRAIL: It is the largest space vessel ever built. Research will be conducted onboard into the long-term effects of space travel on human beings.

How do you like the idea of living in space? Today, this is no longer science fiction. The astronauts and cosmonauts aboard the International Space Station are doing just that. They are living and working in space — for three to six months at a time.

The International Space Station is a facility for space research. This project is the joint effort of numerous international space agencies, such as the National Aeronautics and Space Administration (NASA), the Russian Federal Space Agency (RKA), the Canadian Space Agency (CSA), and the European Space Agency (ESA). Work on the station began in 1998. It is made up of components, or parts, which are put together like a giant jigsaw puzzle. When completed after 10 years, the station will weigh more than one million pounds. It will look like a five-bedroom house — with living quarters, laboratories, and service modules.

The first crew arrived in November 2000. They stayed for 136 days. Since then, there are always at least two crew members living and working aboard the station.

---

cosmonauts: *Russian astronauts*
modules: *sections*

 The partners of this international project are Russia, the United States, Japan, Canada, and several countries belonging to the European Space Agency. All of them participate in different ways. What are the pros and cons of having so many countries involved in a project?

INTERNATIONAL SPACE STATION

This December 2000 photo is one of the first images of the entire International Space Station with its solar panels deployed.

THE MISSION

Orbiting about 225 miles above Earth, the International Space Station has been and will be home to many astronauts. The station will be a permanent laboratory for space research. It will enable scientists to study the effects of long-term space travel on people, machines, and equipment.

INTO THE UNKNOWN

The station is most revolutionary in terms of design and size. When completed, it will be the size of two football fields. It will have more than 100 components, which will take almost 50 space flights to deliver! Building such a massive facility while weightless is another challenge. Imagine trying to tighten a bolt and your wrench floats away. Then there are building delays and rising costs. The project is estimated to take 10 years and will cost $130 billion.

orbiting: *moving around a planet or star*

? Space exploration costs millions and even billions of dollars. Do you think this money could be better spent elsewhere? Explain.

MISSION ACCOMPLISHED

Crews on the station have taken more than 250,000 photographs of Earth and its atmosphere. These photographs provide valuable information about long-term, large-scale changes in the environment. Scientists have also gathered new information about how plants grow in space and how human beings react to weightlessness over a long period. Scientists are interested in knowing how the heart, muscles, bones, arteries, and veins are affected. Research findings will determine if people can someday live their entire lives in space. The information will shape future missions to other planets, such as Mars and the moon.

Quick Fact

The International Space Station orbits Earth approximately every 90 minutes at a speed of 17,500 mph. As of 2006, the station has completed more than 45,000 orbits.

An astronaut working outside the space station

10

9 8 7 6

ALL IMAGES—NASA

PIECES OF THE PUZZLE

This diagram describes some of the most important components of the International Space Station.

Destiny Laboratory
This is a laboratory where astronauts conduct important scientific research. Physics, chemistry, and biology experiments can all be done here. There is also a special facility for testing how people react to weightlessness.

Solar Arrays
These giant solar panels capture the sun's energy and store it in special batteries. This solar power is the main source of electricity for the entire ship.

Resupply Vehicle
This specialized rocket brings supplies from Earth to the station. There are no human passengers, so the rocket is driven by an onboard computer. Supplies can include food, clothing, tools, and fuel.

Canadarm2
This Canadian robotic arm was added to help with construction. It moves modules and astronauts into position to work on the station.

Soyuz Spacecraft
These Russian spacecraft are used to transport astronauts to the International Space Station and back to Earth after their duty in space. At least one *Soyuz* is always at the station to provide a quick escape in case of an emergency. It is very much like the lifeboat of a ship.

The Expert Says...

"Today, NASA is moving forward with a new focus for the manned space program: to go out beyond Earth's orbit for purposes of human exploration and scientific discovery. And the International Space Station is now a stepping stone on the way, rather than being the end of the line.

— Mike Griffin, NASA Administrator

Take Note

Even though the International Space Station is not fully complete, it has already opened the door for experimentation. It serves as a "first step" in learning how to live in space, thereby furthering space discovery. For these reasons, we have ranked the station #10.

• Would you want to live and work in space? What would be the benefits of this? Explain your answers.

5   4   3   2   1

American astronaut Shannon Lucid spent 188 days on Mir in 1996. This was the longest period of time spent by a non-Soviet person.

MIR–NASA

LAUNCH DATE: February 20, 1986

LENGTH OF MISSION: Mir orbited Earth for 15 years.

BLAZING THE TRAIL: Mir was the first permanent space station in orbit.

At a time when the United States and the Soviet Union were at odds on land, they came together in space. In 1986, the Mir Space Station began its 15-year orbit around Earth. It was the first true long-term home in space, where Soviet and American astronauts could live for many months at a time and conduct scientific research.

Mir, a Russian word for peace, was developed by the Soviets. It was made up of seven different modules. Each module was flown into space separately. The station was put together in space and took 10 years to complete.

The station was 140 feet long and weighed 135 tons. It orbited Earth at an altitude ranging between 185 and 250 miles. Inside the station, people floated and traveled through the different modules by pushing themselves through the air. The floor of the living compartment was carpeted, and the walls and ceilings were painted. This helped cosmonauts and astronauts to feel more at home while aboard the station.

Over the years, Mir became more and more prone to accidents and breakdowns. It was removed from orbit in 2001.

MIR SPACE STATION

THE MISSION

Mir was the first long-term research station in space. The objective was to find out the effects of prolonged space flight on the human body. It served as a laboratory for experiments with plants and research in life science and biology.

? Why do you think scientists want to experiment in space?

INTO THE UNKNOWN

The Mir Space Station had its share of disasters. In 1997, two near-fatal accidents occurred. A fire broke out and cosmonauts almost had to leave the station. Luckily, they were able to put out the fire and little damage was done. Later in the year, a cargo ship crashed into the station. A solar panel was damaged, and oxygen leaked into space. The damaged section was quickly sealed off from the rest of the station. After a few other minor mishaps, the decision to abandon Mir was made in 1998. It was removed from orbit three years later. It burned over the Pacific Ocean upon re-entering Earth's atmosphere.

objective: *goal*

Space shuttle Atlantis *undocks from the* Mir *Space Station.*

Quick Fact

Every space traveler must carry a passport, because he or she may land in a foreign country upon returning to Earth.

MISSION ACCOMPLISHED

Mir racked up an impressive number of accomplishments in its lifetime. It set the records for the longest time in orbit for a space station — 15 years; longest time in space for a human — 438 days; and the heaviest object ever to orbit Earth. Mir's biggest contribution was bringing together the world's two superpowers: the Soviet Union and the United States. Mir's research on how equipment and people responded to extended periods in space also helped with the International Space Station program that came later.

Quick Fact

Cosmonaut Dr. Valery Polyakov holds the record for the longest period of time spent in space in 1995. He lived on Mir for 438 days. Those who lived aboard Mir and those who live aboard the International Space Station today are expected to exercise several hours a day to prevent their muscles from weakening.

Mir in orbit

LIVING ON MIR

Sweet dreams! Astronaut Norm Thagard zips into his sleep restraint in the Core Module of the Mir Space Station.

ALL IMAGES—NASA MARSHALL SPACE FLIGHT CENTER (NASA-MSFC)

Living in space can be quite challenging. Daily events that are routine on Earth become more difficult in space. This fact chart describes how astronauts and cosmonauts adapt to their lifestyles in space.

WASHING

On Earth, water flows down, but in orbit, water droplets just float through the weightless environment. This means that the cosmonauts and astronauts on Mir were not able to splash water on their faces or run water for a shower. Water was stored in sealed bags and carefully applied to a washcloth that was used for bathing. Special non-rinse shampoo was used for washing hair. The shampoo was carefully wiped out of the hair using a towel.

TEETH BRUSHING

When cosmonauts or astronauts brushed their teeth, they had to keep their lips tight around the toothbrush. This was so that the toothpaste and saliva in the mouth would not float out into the cabin.

EATING

Both American and Soviet food was available to the cosmonauts and astronauts on Mir. The dehydrated food was stored in a bag and rehydrated using heated water. When eating, the crew members had to be careful that their food did not float away. Drinks were served in drinking bags similar to juice boxes. To prevent the drink from floating out of the bag, special straws that could be opened and closed were used.

SLEEPING

At night, the cosmonauts and astronauts strapped themselves into sleeping bags that were secured to a wall or the floor.

TOILET

Cosmonauts and astronauts had to strap themselves to the toilet. A vacuum system was used to prevent waste from floating away.

The Expert Says...

" Mir has completed its triumphant mission. It was unprecedented in the history of space research. "

— Russian Mission Control Announcer upon the re-entry of Mir into Earth's atmosphere

unprecedented: *never done before*

Take Note

The Mir Space Station takes the #9 spot on the list. It enabled scientists to learn the effects of prolonged space flight on humans and equipment. This information was helpful in the development of the International Space Station. The research findings will also be used to prepare for future flights to Mars and the moon.

- Besides prolonged space flight, what are other issues that scientists might consider when planning future space missions?

5   4   3   2   1

This is an artist's drawing of the Cassini probe that is orbiting Saturn.

PROBE–NASA/JPL

ACE PROBES

LAUNCH DATE: December 1962

LENGTH OF MISSION: The last transmission from the first successful planetary space probe, *Mariner 2*, was on January 3, 1963. Space probes are still used in ongoing missions.

BLAZING THE TRAIL: Space probes have advanced our knowledge of the planets and have collected valuable information safely and efficiently.

Have you ever wondered what other planets in our solar system are like? Do they have forests and large bodies of water? Can we live on them? Thanks to space probes, we are getting a closer look at other planets and learning more about them than ever before.

The first successful planetary space probe was launched in 1962. The probe, named *Mariner 2*, was sent to survey the planet Venus. It collected a lot of valuable information. For instance, scientists once thought Venus was Earth's twin planet because of its cloud cover. We now know that Venus is quite unlike Earth. It is extremely hot and is full of clouds made of acid.

There is so much to learn about our solar system that it's impossible to identify only one successful space probe. Space probe missions can go to planets that are too far away or too dangerous for human beings. Some missions orbit the planets without landing. Others are programmed to land. Whatever they do, planetary space probes have advanced our knowledge of the solar system for over three decades.

PLANETARY SPACE PROBES

THE MISSION

Planetary space probes make it possible for scientists to safely study the solar system. They collect data about planets' surfaces and atmospheres. Some probes do this by using sensors to measure the temperature of a planet. Radars are used to see a planet through clouds. The first probe to orbit Jupiter was *Galileo*, named after the famous astronomer Galileo Galilei. Even more famous than *Galileo* are *Voyager 1* and *Voyager 2*, which were launched in 1977. Both probes are still in space and sending back information.

astronomer: *scientist who studies the universe*

Quick Fact

Pioneer 10 was an American probe sent to survey Jupiter and deep space in 1972. It has traveled over 75.8 billion miles and relayed information back to Earth for over 30 years. The last message was relayed in January 2003.

Pioneer 10

> What type of information would you like a probe to discover if you were to design one to land on a planet?

INTO THE UNKNOWN

It can take a space probe many months or even years to reach its planetary destination. If a part breaks or malfunctions, scientists cannot reach the probe to fix it. The entire mission can be lost. In the 1950s and '60s, many probes failed due to faulty software, damaged equipment, or the pressure from planets' atmospheres.

MISSION ACCOMPLISHED

Each probe that reached a planet has managed to send back to Earth lots of useful information. Scientists are now starting to get a clearer idea of what other planets are really like. They have learned that Mars experiences a change in seasons like Earth. It is most like Earth in that the temperatures are similar and the length of days are almost the same amount of hours. Mars could very well be the first planet to be colonized.

colonized: *settled by humans*

> If Mars were colonized, would you be willing to move there? Why or why not?

Quick Fact

Voyager 2 was launched in 1977. It surveyed Jupiter, Saturn, Uranus, and Neptune and is now traveling into deep space. It has been surveying the solar system for over 30 years and is still going strong.

The Expert Says...

" The amazement is in recognizing that, by exploring space, we are doing something that's never been done before — that we are discovering that there are many interesting things in space. "

— Ellis Miner, Ph.D., NASA planetary scientist

THE PLANETS OF OUR SOLAR SYSTEM

Thanks to planetary space probes, scientists have photographs and a wealth of information about other planets in our solar system. Check out the diagram below.

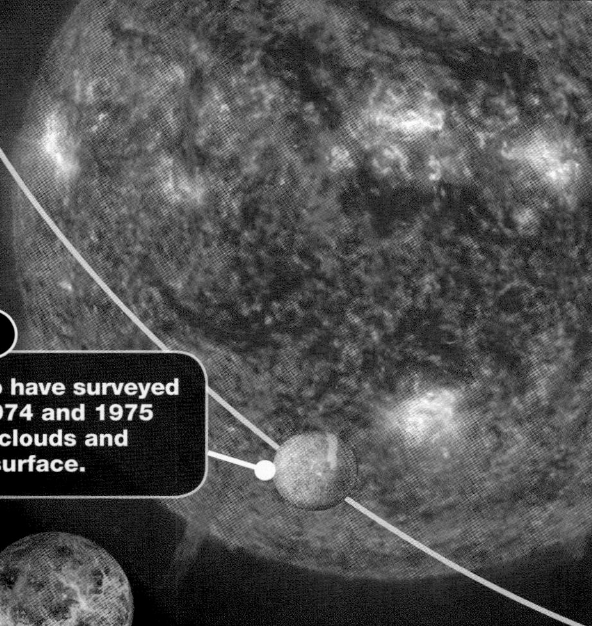

Mercury

Mariner 10 is the only probe to have surveyed Mercury. Photographs from 1974 and 1975 revealed evidence of rotating clouds and showed many craters on the surface.

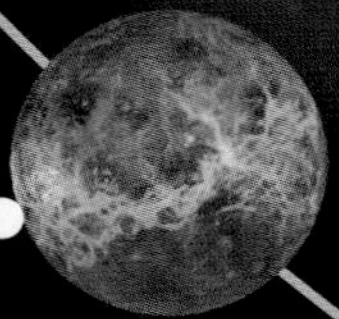

Venus

Mariner 2 was the first successful probe to observe Venus in 1962. Other probes have shown that Venus has thousands of active volcanoes and many mountain ranges. The surface temperature is over 900°F.

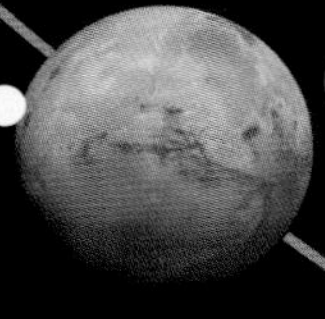

Mars

Mariner 4 took the first images of Mars in 1965. **Mariner 9** returned even more information, revealing large volcanoes, giant canyons, and evidence that water once flowed across this planet.

Earth

Quick Fact

Three guidelines are used to define a planet. A planet must be big enough to form into a ball; must orbit the sun; and must be able to clear other objects out of the way while orbiting. Pluto was downsized to a dwarf planet in 2006 because it did not fulfill the third guideline.

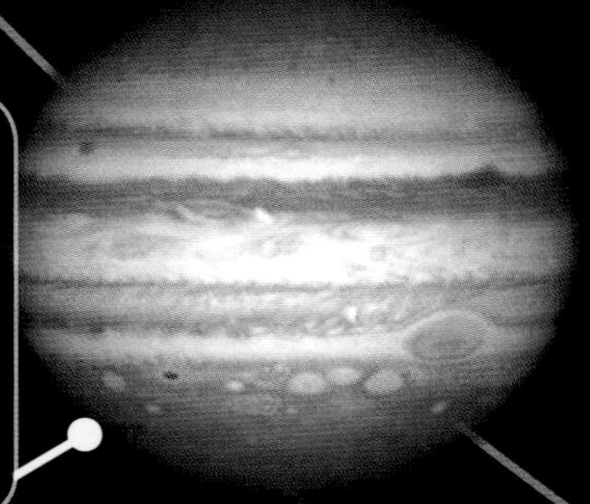

Jupiter

Galileo circled Jupiter 34 times and sent more than 14,000 pictures of the planet to Earth. It provided evidence that three of Jupiter's moons, Europa, Callisto, and Ganymede all have sub-surface water.

Saturn

Voyagers 1 and **2** flew by Saturn and discovered it has over 1,000 rings and seven satellites. The **Cassini-Huygens** probe is the first to orbit Saturn. It has gathered information on the planet's magnetic field and its many moons. This probe will examine Saturn until 2008.

Uranus

Voyager 2 is the only probe to have flown past Uranus. In 1986, it took photographs of the planet's rings and discovered 10 new moons.

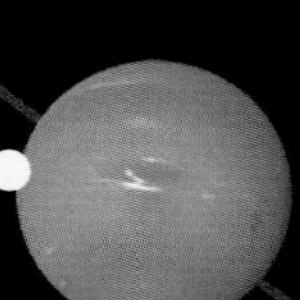

Neptune

In 1989, **Voyager 2** became the only probe to survey Neptune. Six new moons were found. Large storms were observed on the planet.

Take Note

Space probes fly into the #8 spot. Mir contributed valuable information about the long-term effects on humans living in space. However, planetary space probes have allowed scientists to make closer observations than ever before of other planets in our solar system. These could be planets that we will inhabit one day.

- Do you think it is important that we find out more about the solar system? Why?

Pluto

Very little is known about Pluto. The probe called **New Horizons** was launched January 2006 and will reach Pluto by 2015.

SIMPLE PROBE–ISTOCKPHOTO; PIONEER 10 ART–NASA/ARC; VOYAGER 2–NASA/MSFC; ELLIS MINER–NASA; PLANETS–NASA/LUNAR AND PLANETARY LABORATORY

5   4   3   2   1

7 SOJOURNER

Sojourner was expected to operate only for a week. Instead, it traveled Mars for three months.

MARS ROVER—NASA/JPL

ROVER

LAUNCH DATE: Launched December 4, 1996 and landed July 4, 1997

LENGTH OF MISSION: From July 4 to September 27, 1997

BLAZING THE TRAIL: The *Sojourner* rover was the very first mobile robotic vehicle to reach Mars.

You can see the planet Mars from Earth with your naked eye. Try looking for it in the night sky. It is called the Red Planet because its reddish soil gives it a red appearance.

Mars is like Earth in many ways — it has craters, mountains, and canyons. It has the same seasonal cycles, and water most likely once flowed across the planet. Scientists are fascinated by Mars not only because it is similar to Earth, but also because there is a possibility that life once existed on this planet.

The *Mars Pathfinder* mission in 1996 was the first of its kind. It transported the very first mobile robotic rover to Mars. Called *Sojourner*, the rover was a six-wheeled vehicle that could drive over rocky terrain and smooth surfaces. Controlled and steered by scientists on Earth, *Sojourner* drove off from the *Mars Pathfinder* and explored the planet Mars for three months. It took hundreds of photographs and gathered rock and soil samples. *Sojourner* provided scientists with a great deal of information about the Red Planet.

SOJOURNER ROVER

Mars Pathfinder landed in an area called Ares Vallis.

THE MISSION

The *Sojourner* rover was launched in 1996 to explore Mars. Scientists wanted more data to determine whether humans could inhabit Mars in the future. *Mars Pathfinder* landed in an area called Ares Vallis (Air-eez Val-lees). It is an ancient flood plain on Mars's northern hemisphere. *Sojourner* had much to do. It had to take photographs, drill rocks, and analyze soil samples.

flood plain: *flat land once covered with water*

Quick Fact

Sojourner means traveler. The *Sojourner* rover weighed about 25 pounds and was two feet long. Its six wheels were five inches across and made of aluminium.

A group of engineers make adjustments to a Mars exploration rover.

INTO THE UNKNOWN

On landing, *Mars Pathfinder* lowered a set of wheel ramps and *Sojourner* rolled down the ramps onto the surface of Mars. Mars is a very cold planet with an average temperature of around -76°F. *Sojourner* was designed to withstand the cold weather and storms and to climb over rough terrain without getting stuck. All the information it collected was sent to *Mars Pathfinder* to relay back to Earth. *Mars Pathfinder* and *Sojourner* used energy from solar panels to keep working for almost three months on Mars.

? What more would you want to know about Mars?

MISSION ACCOMPLISHED

The mission produced more than 17,000 images and as many as 15 chemical analyses of rocks and soil samples. This mission was proof that rovers could be used to explore the planet. *Sojourner* and *Mars Pathfinder* ran out of battery power after a few months. As a result of this mission, larger rovers were built to last much longer. The rovers *Spirit* and *Opportunity* landed on Mars in 2004. They are still sending information back to Earth.

 ? What would you use to gather information: rovers or space probes? Explain.

PHOTO FROM MARS–NASA/JPL/CALTECH/CORNELL; ALL IMAGES–NASA/JPL

THE LOST ROVER

A Web article from NewScientist.com
By Maggie McKee, January 12, 2007

The most powerful camera ever sent into orbit around Mars has spotted yet another lander lying lifeless on its surface: *Mars Pathfinder*, which operated for three months in 1997. It may also have found the mission's tiny rover, *Sojourner*, which appears to have crawled toward *Pathfinder* after the lander had already died. …

But despite MRO's [Mars Reconnaissance Orbiter] sharp eyesight, it is still not clear whether it has spied *Sojourner*, the toaster oven-sized rover that hitched a ride to the planet's surface inside the lander, then struck out to explore its surroundings.

Unlike *Spirit* and *Opportunity*, *Sojourner* could not directly communicate with Earth and had to rely on the lander to transmit messages about its health and travels. So when contact with the lander, which was designed to last one month, was lost after three months, ground controllers were not sure what became of *Sojourner*.

Now, it seems the rover kept moving, apparently trying to reach its companion. "The rover was programmed so that if it didn't get commands from the lander, it would assume it somehow got out of radio contact behind a ridge or rock," [NASA geologist Tim] Parker told NewScientist. "So it would drive to the lander as best it could and keep trying to re-establish contact," circling it as it got close, he says. …

Still, the images are not clear enough to definitively identify the rover, and Parker says what the team is seeing may just be a cluster of pebbles. So they have considered the possibility that the rover simply drove off on its own after its partner died. …

Mars Reconnaissance Orbiter: *launched by NASA and entered Mars's orbit on March 10, 2006*

The Expert Says…

" Part of exploration is confronting the unknown, and risk can never be removed completely. In cases like *Pathfinder*, taking a little risk can result in an enormous payoff. "

— Dr. Matthew Golombek, project scientist of the Jet Propulsion Laboratory

Take Note

Sojourner roams into the #7 spot on our list. Although planetary space probes provide us with information about planets, *Sojourner* was the first rover to drive on the surface of another planet. Its success has helped scientists to learn more about the Red Planet.

• NASA's goal is to land a person on Mars by 2012. Do you support this type of space mission? What might be the payoff?

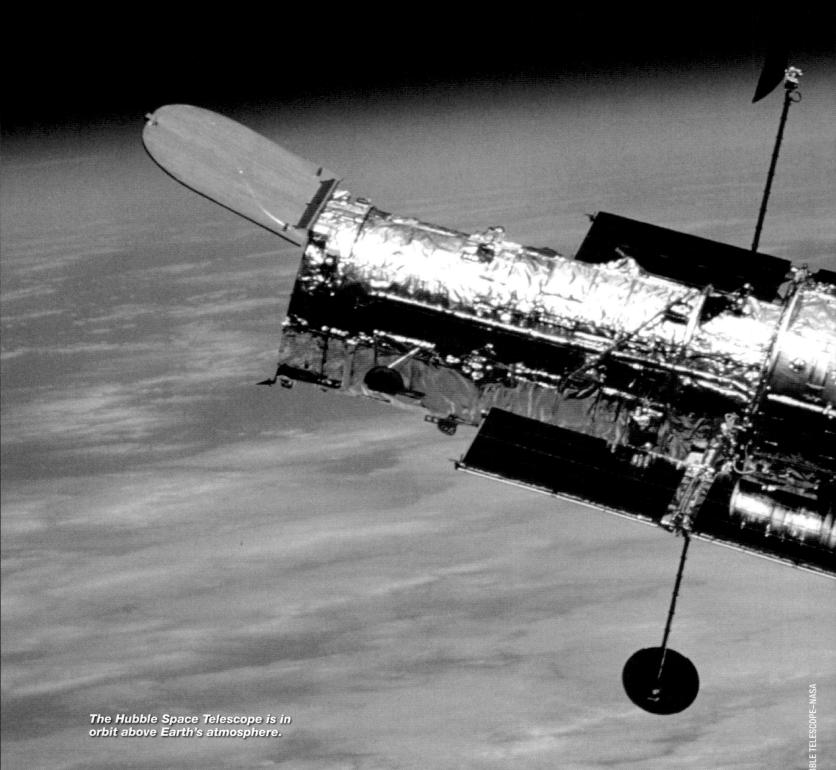

The Hubble Space Telescope is in orbit above Earth's atmosphere.

HUBBLE TELESCOPE–NASA

TELESCOPE

LAUNCH DATE: April 24, 1990

LENGTH OF MISSION: Scheduled to remain in orbit through 2013

BLAZING THE TRAIL: This powerful telescope gives us tremendous images of distant galaxies and has provided thousands of images of deep space.

What many of us know about the universe is what we've learned from Earth-bound telescopes. But things are changing now that we have the Hubble Space Telescope in space.

This giant optical telescope orbits about 360 miles above Earth's atmosphere. This position allows it to have a better view of the universe in order to see images clearly because they are not blurred by the atmosphere. The telescope weighs 25,575 pounds and is about the size of a tractor-trailer truck. It is so powerful that it can look deep into the universe. It can discover stars, galaxies, and comets that are new to us. It can capture cosmic events and transmit images to Earth instantly. Nothing escapes the watchful eye of the Hubble. We are learning so much more about the universe than ever before, thanks to the Hubble mission.

Scientists use satellite signals to control Hubble and use multiple antennae to transmit information to Earth. Hubble is one of NASA's most successful breakthroughs in space exploration.

***

optical: *having to do with sight and light*

HUBBLE SPACE TELESCOPE

THE MISSION

For centuries, scientists and astronomers have been curious about what happens in the universe. Hubble is providing scientists with information they need. This giant telescope completes a spin around Earth every 97 minutes. As it travels, Hubble's mirrors capture light and direct it into several scientific instruments. Then, these images are sent back to Earth for scientists to study and analyze.

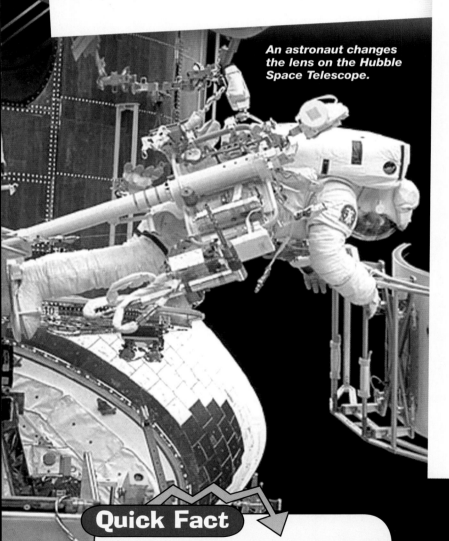

An astronaut changes the lens on the Hubble Space Telescope.

Quick Fact

The James Webb Space Telescope will replace Hubble. It is scheduled to launch in 2013 and will orbit about one million miles from Earth.

INTO THE UNKNOWN

The first images from the Hubble Space Telescope were blurry. A tiny flaw with the main mirror distorted the view. Astronauts and the NASA crew trained for almost a year to fix the problem. The astronauts also repaired a broken solar panel. Since its launch in 1990, Hubble has been serviced and repaired many times. The final service of the Hubble Space Telescope is due in 2008. Its parts will break down by 2013.

Quick Fact

The Hubble Space Telescope was named after the famous astronomer Edwin Hubble. In the 1920s, at the Mount Wilson Observatory in California, he proved the existence of galaxies beyond our own.

MISSION ACCOMPLISHED

Hubble has returned hundreds of thousands of photographs to Earth. This information has helped scientists to determine that the universe is about 13 to 14 billion years old. Observations from Hubble suggest the existence of dark energy. Scientists cannot see dark energy, but some believe it is speeding up the expansion of the universe. This amazing telescope has seen galaxies well over 12 billion light-years away. More than 6,000 articles have been published based on the Hubble data.

light-years: *units of 5.87 trillion miles, which is the distance that light travels in one year*

Why do you think scientists want to learn more about the universe? How can this knowledge be beneficial to all of us?

ALL IMAGES—NASA

OUT OF THIS WORLD

The Hubble Space Telescope is located about 360 miles above Earth's atmosphere. It is 43.5 feet in length and 14 feet wide. Hubble has taken some of the most beautiful photographs in the universe, as you can see in this photo essay.

This galaxy is about 69 million light-years from Earth. Bright star clusters are highlighted in red, and clouds of dust are blue. This image was taken in September 2004.

This image shows a bubbly ocean of gases clumping to form stars. The colors represent various gases: red for sulphur, green for hydrogen, and blue for oxygen. This image was taken in May 1999.

This bright red star is located near the edge of our Milky Way galaxy. The brown halo is probably dust and other matter that escaped from the star after it exploded. This image was taken in February 2004.

Take Note

The Hubble Space Telescope has taught us more about the universe than any other scientific equipment. Although the *Sojourner* rover provided scientists with information about Mars, the Hubble Space Telescope has returned information about the entire universe. It holds the #6 spot on our list.

- Go online to see images of the Hubble Space Telescope. What do you find most impressive about this project?

The Expert Says...

"Hubble has been rewriting astronomy textbooks for more than 15 years, and all of us are looking forward to the new chapters that will be added with future discoveries and insights about our universe.

— Mary Cleave, NASA's Associate Administrator for the Science Mission Directorate

Without the original Canadarm, this newer and more sophisticated Canadarm2 would never have been conceived.

CANADARM2–NASA

LAUNCH DATE: November 13, 1981

LENGTH OF MISSION: Ongoing

BLAZING THE TRAIL: The Canadarm has been involved in many key space missions for more than 25 years.

The Canadian Space Agency (CSA) can take credit for one of the greatest successes in space exploration: the Canadarm. This mechanical arm is also called the Remote Manipulator System. It was first put to use in 1981.

The Canadarm functions like a human arm to help astronauts move very large objects in space. It has nerves of copper wiring, bones of graphite fiber, and electric motors for muscles. It has a shoulder, an elbow, and a wrist. Each part has rotating joints to allow it to move easily. The entire arm is 50 feet long and weighs 905 pounds. It is wrapped with a special blanket to protect it from the heat of the sun and the cold temperature in space.

An astronaut inside a space shuttle controls the arm. The Canadarm is strong, flexible, and mobile. It was designed to have a lifetime of only 10 years. More than 25 years and 70 missions later, the Canadarm is still functioning as well as it did on the day it was created! It is one of the most useful tools in space exploration.

CANADARM

THE MISSION

NASA needed an affordable, safe, and effective way of moving large pieces of equipment during missions in space. NASA turned to the CSA, which created a robotic piece of technology that functioned like a human arm. The Canadarm has been useful in many ways. It assists astronauts during space walks, sets and retrieves satellites from space, and moves cargo.

Quick Fact

The Canadarm was used to install the Canadarm2 on the International Space Station. The Canadarm2 in turn was used to assemble the International Space Station.

INTO THE UNKNOWN

Naturally, it would be somewhat of a challenge for astronauts to maneuver a giant arm in space. It must be moved slowly and accurately. It can only reach so far because of its length, and it has no sense of touch. However, the Canadarm has never failed a mission and has required very few repairs all these years.

MISSION ACCOMPLISHED

The Canadarm can lift and move objects that weigh more than 66,000 pounds, equivalent to a bus. It has participated in over 70 space missions, and it has launched, repaired, and captured many satellites. The Canadarm helped set the Hubble Space Telescope into orbit in 1990. It has helped with the docking of space shuttles to the Mir Space Station. In one space shuttle mission, the Canadarm removed an ice growth that had formed on the shuttle, helping to prevent an accident. Canadarm also assisted in attaching Canadarm2 to the International Space Station's Destiny laboratory in 2001.

? How can a robotic arm like the Canadarm be used on Earth? Think of all the various uses for a robotic arm on land.

Astronaut Chris Hadfield is seen near the Canadarm2.

The Expert Says...

"Its remarkable performance produced a rush of relief and joy. We had done everything possible to make it work, but we had never been able to test it in a space environment. Seeing the arm deployed without a hitch showed that the eight years of hard work had paid off with a spectacular success."

— Dr. Garry Lindberg, first program manager for Canadarm

deployed: *positioned*

CANADARM IMAGES–NASA–MSFC BACKGROUND–SHUTTERSTOCK

CANADA
and the International Space Station
*An **article** from CBC News, January 15, 2006*

The International Space Station is seen here with the Canadarm2.

Astronaut Scott Parazynski is anchored to the end of the Canadarm2 as he attaches a critical part of the station's electrical system.

The International Space Station is an orbiting science lab, a multibillion-dollar construction project, and the most massive artificial object ever to orbit the Earth. ...

Canada's major contribution is known to NASA as the Space Station Remote Manipulator System, but it's better known as Canadarm2. ...

Canadarm2 is a larger and more sophisticated version of the robotic arm built for the space shuttle. Fully extended, the arm is nearly 18 metres [59 feet] long, three metres [10 feet] longer than the shuttle's arm, and can handle loads up to 116 tonnes [128 tons].

The new arm also has a hand on either end so one can latch onto the space station while the other end reaches out and picks up things that it needs. Then it can let go and grab on somewhere else.

The real talent in the new design is in its ability to move around where the astronauts most need the robot arm. The Canadarm2 can crawl along the body of the space station on its two hands, end over end like an inchworm. The outside of the station has a number of sockets where the arm can plug in. As well, the arm can be fixed to a work platform that moves on rails from one end of the station to the other.

Canada is also planning to contribute a smaller, two-armed robot that has finer movements than either of the arms. It's designed to take on delicate assembly jobs that are now done by astronauts on space walks. ...

Take Note

The Canadarm takes the #5 spot on our list. It is one of the most remarkable technological inventions in space history. It is used to deploy, capture, and repair satellites and space vehicles. It helped to install the Canadarm2, which is part of the International Space Station's mobile system.

• If you could interview an astronaut who has operated the Canadarm, what three questions would you ask him or her about the robotic arm?

5   4   3   2   1

COLUMBIA–NASA

USA

Columbia *was named after the first American ocean vessel to circle the globe in 1790.*

ACE SHUTTLE

LAUNCH DATE: April 12, 1981

LENGTH OF MISSION: Two days, ended on April 14, 1981

BLAZING THE TRAIL: *Columbia* was the first reusable crewed spacecraft to be launched into orbit.

Since the 1960s, space exploration has made great progress. Astronauts have been into space, walked on the moon, and completed space walks outside Earth's atmosphere. But each time, the capsule that took the crew into space could not be reused. That's when NASA decided to build a shuttle that could be flown again and again, like an airplane. From that idea, space shuttle *Columbia* was born.

Construction of the shuttle began in 1975. Two years later, the shuttle arrived at the John F. Kennedy Space Center in Florida to prepare for its first launch. It would take another two years to get it ready. On April 12, 1981, Commander John Young and Pilot Robert Crippen strapped into the 85.7-ton vessel and prepared for takeoff.

At 7:00 AM Eastern Standard Time, space shuttle *Columbia* made its first launch into space. Eight minutes later, it was orbiting Earth at 17,000 miles per hour. *Columbia* became the first reusable space shuttle and the first shuttle to orbit Earth.

COLUMBIA SPACE SHUTTLE

Once back on Earth, a space shuttle is returned to the Kennedy Space Center on the back of a specially designed Boeing 747 jet.

THE MISSION

The mission was to build a space shuttle that could be used more than once. This would save millions of dollars that each shuttle cost. *Columbia's* cutting-edge technology made it a piece of art. Fully fueled, the entire space shuttle weighed over four million pounds.

INTO THE UNKNOWN

Scientists spend a great deal of time making sure space shuttles are safe for travel. Earth's atmosphere is very thick and can cause massive damage to the shuttle if it's not flown properly in and out of the atmosphere. The pilot maneuvers the shuttle carefully so it does not enter the atmosphere nose first. During *Columbia's* first launch, the shuttle suffered tile damage from the blast created by the solid rocket boosters. These tiles help protect the shuttle from the extreme heat caused by entering the atmosphere. Sixteen tiles were lost and 148 damaged.

MISSION ACCOMPLISHED

Columbia spent almost 55 hours in flight and orbited Earth 36 times. Astronaut John Young then guided the shuttle to Edwards Air Force Base in California. It was a perfect landing. Young and Crippen accomplished more than 130 flight test objectives. Since 1981, *Columbia* made 28 flights and completed about 4,800 orbits. Unfortunately, on February 1, 2003, Columbia was destroyed upon re-entering Earth's atmosphere. The seven-passenger crew died in the accident.

 Knowing the dangers of space travel, would you want to become an astronaut? Why or why not?

Quick Fact

The space shuttle is made up of four main parts: the orbiter (which is the shuttle), one external fuel tank, and two solid rocket boosters. The external tank is destroyed during launch, but the orbiter and solid rocket boosters can be reused on many missions. The external tank holds almost 530,000 gallons of liquid fuel.

Main Engines

Vertical Stabilizer

Payload Bay Doors

Crew Cabin

United States

USA

Body Flap

Wing

ALL IMAGES—NASA

10   8   7   6

SHUTTLES IN SPACE

The space shuttle *Atlantis* receives post-flight servicing after a successful landing on June 22, 2007.

Columbia wasn't the only space shuttle to make history or accomplish important goals. Check out the launch dates of other NASA space shuttles in the fact chart below. More than 300 astronauts and cosmonauts have flown aboard these shuttles over the years.

April 4, 1983: *Challenger*

In June 1983, *Challenger* carried the first American woman, Sally Ride, into space. It also carried an IMAX movie camera into space to film spectacular space footage. A *Challenger* expedition ended in tragedy on January 28, 1986 when the shuttle exploded only a minute after takeoff.

August 30, 1984: *Discovery*

Discovery is the third of NASA's fleet. It carried the Hubble Space Telescope into space in 1990. It transported crews to perform maintenance on the telescope in 1997 and 1999. *Discovery* has also carried several portions of the International Space Station into orbit.

October 3, 1985: *Atlantis*

Atlantis was the fourth shuttle to be built. It carried the *Galileo* and *Magellan* space probes. It was also the first shuttle to carry astronauts to the Mir Space Station.

May 7, 1992: *Endeavour*

Endeavour is NASA's fifth shuttle. It was built to replace the ill-fated *Challenger*. *Endeavour* has been involved in many important missions including the repair of the INTELSAT IV communications satellite. Three astronauts spacewalked at the same time (normally only two go) to replace the broken motor in the satellite.

 All of the shuttles are named after ocean vessels. What do space exploration and ocean exploration have in common?

The Expert Says...

" You just had to be there to hear, even feel, the double crack of the sonic boom. It was such a tremendous sense of excitement to see something never seen before, to witness such a historic event. "

— James Young, Chief Historian of the Air Force Flight Test Center at Edwards Air Force Base

sonic boom: *noise made when an aircraft travels faster than the speed of sound*

Take Note

The space shuttle is responsible for bringing many astronauts and equipment into space. It has enabled many satellites, probes, and telescopes to be placed in orbit and the International Space Station to be built. The shuttle has continued to play an important role in space missions. It takes the #4 spot on our list.

• What space mission would you like NASA to undertake? Think about the main goal, the destination, the spacecraft, and the crew size.

5 **4** 3 2 1

A replica of a Sputnik satellite is on display at the Smithsonian Air and Space Museum in Washington, D.C.

SPUTNIK 1—© BETTMANN/CORBIS

TELLITES

LAUNCH DATE: October 4, 1957

LENGTH OF MISSION: Ongoing — satellites are still used to provide scientists with information about space and Earth, but now they are also used for commercial purposes, such as transmitting phone and TV signals.

BLAZING THE TRAIL: It was a race between the United States and the Soviet Union to get the first satellite into space and orbit Earth.

In the 1950s, the Soviet Union and the United States were involved in a space race. Both nations wanted to be the first to launch a satellite into Earth orbit. The Soviets took the lead when they successfully launched *Sputnik 1* on October 4, 1957.

A month later, the Soviets launched another satellite, *Sputnik 2*. This mission was even more significant — the satellite carried a passenger: Laika, a dog. Laika was the very first living creature to orbit Earth. Unfortunately, she was also the first to die in orbit. The Soviets had no way of bringing *Sputnik 2* safely back to Earth.

This technological achievement stunned the world. The fact that a satellite could orbit Earth was incredibly important to scientists. It meant humans could go to space and not depend on telescopes to learn about the universe. Laika also proved that a living being could survive in space. The next step was to send an astronaut to space and back again.

Sending a satellite and a dog into space was a major victory in the area of space exploration. It marked the beginning of a new era: the space age.

 Research why the Soviet Union and the United States were involved in a space race. After all that has been accomplished, who do you think won this race?

THE MISSION

Launching a satellite into space was an incredible space mission that made history. The satellite was *Sputnik 1*. The Soviets attached *Sputnik 1* to a rocket. It carried a thermometer and two radio transmitters, sending data back to scientists on Earth.

INTO THE UNKNOWN

Then the Soviets launched a second satellite, *Sputnik 2*, which carried a living creature, Laika the dog, onboard. For the first few hours after the launch of *Sputnik 2*, Laika's heart beat normally, cabin pressure stayed steady, and the oxygen levels remained constant. It was a triumph for scientists. At the time, scientists did not know how to bring the satellite back. Any spacecraft re-entering Earth's atmosphere would burst into a fiery ball due to friction with the atmosphere.

MISSION ACCOMPLISHED

Sputnik 1 weighed 185 pounds and traveled about 37.3 million miles. *Sputnik 2* weighed over a thousand pounds and was constructed in one month. It completed 2,370 orbits and traveled about 62 million miles. By 1960, scientists were able to return spacecrafts and animals to Earth safely. Strelka and Belka, who were aboard *Sputnik 5*, were the first dogs to come home from space.

? Do you think that animals should be used as test pilots in space exploration? Explain your position.

Laika is seen inside Sputnik 2.

This is a replica of Sputnik 1.

Quick Fact

Soviet scientists aren't sure exactly when Laika died. Many believe that the batteries maintaining Laika's oxygen stopped working after four days, and Laika died soon after.

10　　**9**　　**8**　　**7**　　**6**

A DECADE OF THE SPACE RACE

During the 1950s, the race to launch the first satellite into space began. The timeline below shows the stages of this race.

LAIKA—© MARC GARANGER/CORBIS; SPUTNIK—TIMOTHY VOGEL; VANGUARD1—NASA/GRC; EXPLORER1—NASA/JPL; BACKGROUND—SHUTTERSTOCK

1952 The International Council of Scientific Unions establishes July 1, 1957 to December 31, 1958 as the International Geophysical Year (IGY). During this time scientists around the world would coordinate studies they had conducted in space.

1954 The Council announces its plan to launch an artificial satellite during the IGY to map Earth's surface.

July 1955 The White House announces its plan to launch an Earth-orbiting satellite called *Vanguard* during the IGY.

October 1957 The Soviet Union launches *Sputnik 1*; the U.S. is taken by surprise.

November 1957 Less than a month later, the Soviets launch *Sputnik 2* with Laika aboard.

December 1957 The U.S. launches *Vanguard*. The rocket loses power and *Vanguard* fails to take off after rising a few feet.

January 1958 The U.S. launches *Explorer 1*, its first satellite to orbit Earth.

October 1958 The U.S. steps up its space program to land an astronaut on the moon.

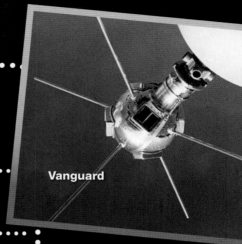

Vanguard

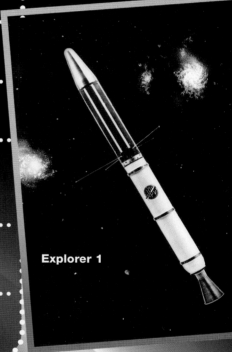

Explorer 1

The Expert Says...

"We thought that if we postponed and postponed we would be second to the U.S. in the space race, so we made the simplest satellite ... with only one reason, to be first in space.

— Gyorgi Grechko, Soviet engineer and cosmonaut

Take Note

The *Sputnik* satellites and Laika's trip marked the beginning of the space age. *Sputnik 2* proved that living things could survive space travel. These missions grasped the attention of the public and kicked off intense research into technologies that would permit human space exploration. For this they fly into the #3 spot.

• The U.S. and the Soviets were engaged in a space race during the 1950s. In what ways do you think the competition helped or hindered space exploration?

3

5   4   3   2   1

② APOLLO 11

Astronaut Neil Armstrong snapped this photo of Edwin "Buzz" Aldrin descending the steps of the lunar module as he prepared to walk on the moon. Armstrong took most of the photos during this historic mission — so he didn't appear in very many!

ALDRIN–NASA

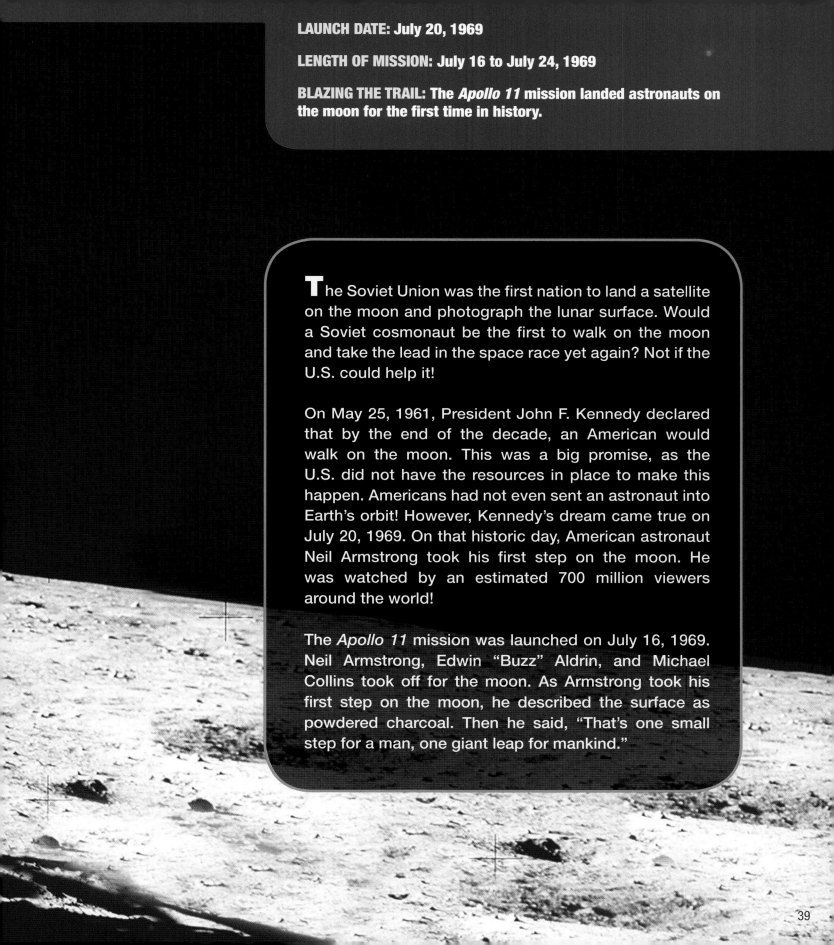

LAUNCH DATE: July 20, 1969

LENGTH OF MISSION: July 16 to July 24, 1969

BLAZING THE TRAIL: The *Apollo 11* mission landed astronauts on the moon for the first time in history.

The Soviet Union was the first nation to land a satellite on the moon and photograph the lunar surface. Would a Soviet cosmonaut be the first to walk on the moon and take the lead in the space race yet again? Not if the U.S. could help it!

On May 25, 1961, President John F. Kennedy declared that by the end of the decade, an American would walk on the moon. This was a big promise, as the U.S. did not have the resources in place to make this happen. Americans had not even sent an astronaut into Earth's orbit! However, Kennedy's dream came true on July 20, 1969. On that historic day, American astronaut Neil Armstrong took his first step on the moon. He was watched by an estimated 700 million viewers around the world!

The *Apollo 11* mission was launched on July 16, 1969. Neil Armstrong, Edwin "Buzz" Aldrin, and Michael Collins took off for the moon. As Armstrong took his first step on the moon, he described the surface as powdered charcoal. Then he said, "That's one small step for a man, one giant leap for mankind."

APOLLO 11

The U.S. plans to land another astronaut on the moon by 2018.

THE MISSION

When the Soviet Union launched the first satellite in 1957, the U.S. knew it had to speed up its space program. The *Apollo 11* mission made history when it landed on the moon. Armstrong and Aldrin were the first two astronauts to walk on the lunar surface. They photographed the surface and took soil and rock samples.

? Put your science skills to the test! What kind of facts do you think can be learned by studying a moon rock?

Quick Fact

Each *Apollo* crew consisted of three astronauts. Two from each mission would walk on the moon while the third remained in the spacecraft orbiting the moon. The *Apollo* capsule was designed to land in the ocean on its return to Earth.

Armstrong   Collins   Aldrin

INTO THE UNKNOWN

When the U.S. took on the challenge of putting an astronaut on the moon, there was no rocket or vessel to accomplish such a mission. Thousands of people across America worked tirelessly with new technologies to prepare for the moon mission. They developed new spacesuits, rockets, and scientific equipment. The spacesuits were equipped with a portable life-support system that controlled oxygen, temperature, and pressure.

MISSION ACCOMPLISHED

The moon landing was a victory for the United States. Armstrong and Aldrin planted an American flag. They also left a plaque with former President Richard Nixon's signature and a message stating, "Here men from the planet Earth first set foot upon the moon July 1969 A.D. We came in peace for all mankind." The astronauts collected over 2,000 lunar rocks and soil samples.

Quick Fact

Astronauts from *Apollo 11*, *12*, and *14* were placed in quarantine when they returned to Earth, just in case they brought home any lunar germs. After these missions, the quarantine period was deemed unnecessary.

quarantine: *isolation*

ALL IMAGES—NASA

10   9   8   7   6

Destination: The Moon!

Check out this timeline of Apollo missions.

Apollo 11, July 1969

The first mission to the moon landed in an area called the Sea of Tranquillity. Two astronauts explored the surface for two and a half hours.

Apollo 12, November 1969

The second mission to the moon landed on the Ocean of Storms. The astronauts did experiments, took photographs, and retrieved samples from the *Surveyor 3* spacecraft that had landed on the moon two and a half years earlier.

Apollo 13, April 1970

This mission to the moon ended early when an oxygen tank exploded during flight. The explosion damaged the service module and cut down oxygen and power supplies. Fortunately, the command module systems remained functional, and the crew returned to Earth alive.

Ocean: *dark lowland plains on the surface of the moon*

Apollo 14, February 1971

The third mission used "modularized equipment transport" (a hand-pulled moon wagon) to carry equipment and samples. The astronauts walked on the moon for more than nine hours. One of them was Alan Shepard, who was also the first American in space. He did something memorable — he hit a golf ball across the lunar surface!

Apollo 15, July 1971

Astronauts from the fourth mission drove across the moon surface using the Lunar Rover, which is a vehicle designed for the moon. The Lunar Rover could travel at speeds up to 110 miles per hour.

Apollo 16, April 1972

This moon mission landed in the Cayley Formation, which is a small crater. Astronauts spent almost three days on the surface. Using the Lunar Rover, they carried out experiments, collected samples, and explored a mountain and crater.

Apollo 17, December 1972

This was the final mission to the moon with astronauts aboard. They landed in Littrow Valley and used a Lunar Rover to explore the area.

The Expert Says...

"If somebody'd said before the flight, 'Are you going to get carried away looking at the Earth from the moon?' I would have said, 'No, no way.' But yet when I first looked back at the Earth, standing on the moon, I cried.

— Alan Shepard, commander of *Apollo 14*

Take Note

The *Apollo 11* mission takes the #2 spot on our list. This mission made history — with the first astronaut walk on the moon. It was a defining moment in the 20th century.
• Why do you think NASA has not sent a mission to the moon since 1972?

5   4   3   **2**   1

1 VOSTOK 1

Cosmonaut Yuri Gagarin was the first person to go into outer space.

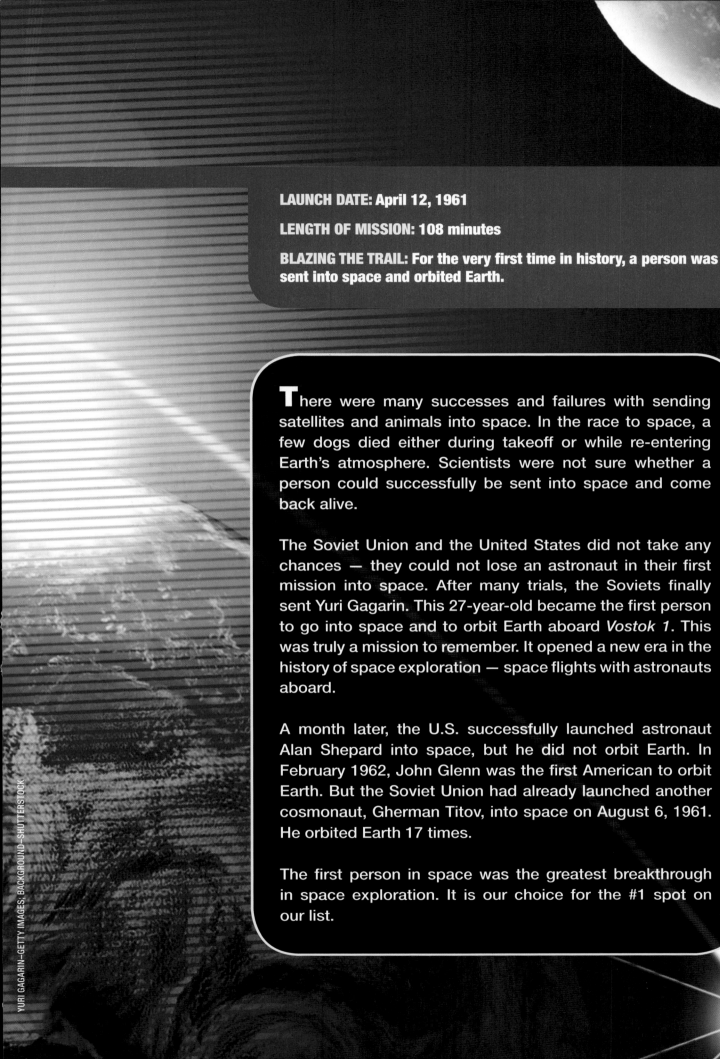

LAUNCH DATE: April 12, 1961

LENGTH OF MISSION: 108 minutes

BLAZING THE TRAIL: For the very first time in history, a person was sent into space and orbited Earth.

There were many successes and failures with sending satellites and animals into space. In the race to space, a few dogs died either during takeoff or while re-entering Earth's atmosphere. Scientists were not sure whether a person could successfully be sent into space and come back alive.

The Soviet Union and the United States did not take any chances — they could not lose an astronaut in their first mission into space. After many trials, the Soviets finally sent Yuri Gagarin. This 27-year-old became the first person to go into space and to orbit Earth aboard *Vostok 1*. This was truly a mission to remember. It opened a new era in the history of space exploration — space flights with astronauts aboard.

A month later, the U.S. successfully launched astronaut Alan Shepard into space, but he did not orbit Earth. In February 1962, John Glenn was the first American to orbit Earth. But the Soviet Union had already launched another cosmonaut, Gherman Titov, into space on August 6, 1961. He orbited Earth 17 times.

The first person in space was the greatest breakthrough in space exploration. It is our choice for the #1 spot on our list.

YURI GAGARIN–GETTY IMAGES; BACKGROUND–SHUTTERSTOCK

VOSTOK 1

THE MISSION

After putting a satellite and a dog into orbit, the next logical step was to send a person into space. Once again, the Soviets beat the U.S. in this race. Yuri Gagarin launched into orbit in *Vostok 1*, traveling at close to 17,000 mph. He orbited Earth in 108 minutes. At the highest point, he was 203 miles above Earth.

A *Vostok* spacecraft is assembled by a number of Soviet technicians.

Many of the early space travelers were pilots. Why do you think people with this profession were chosen for the job? What other attributes would help to take on such a mission?

Quick Fact

The Soviet cosmonauts flew to space in vessels named *Vostok*. The Americans flew in vessels called *Mercury*. The Americans sent chimpanzees into space in the *Mercury* vessels before sending humans.

Quick Fact

Gagarin met some unexpected situations during his time in space. For example, while returning to Earth, the strap that connected the service module to the space capsule failed to separate during landing. It was a wild ride for Gargarin until the strap burned up during reentry.

INTO THE UNKNOWN

Space scientists from the two superpowers were under extreme political pressure to send a human into space. Despite the pressure, adequate safety measures were taken to make the launch and mission safe and successful. Gagarin was not allowed to operate the controls during his orbit. Scientists were unsure how weightlessness and space would affect him. Ground crews controlled the entire mission. Gagarin was not allowed to land *Vostok 1* on his own.

MISSION ACCOMPLISHED

The Soviets were the first to send a person into space, but both superpowers were successful in their crewed space missions. Their missions proved that humans could survive while weightless. In the race to win, the Soviets displayed commitment and determination to engage in further space research and exploration. Putting humans in orbit was the first bold and daring step in paving the way for future human space missions.

How do you think Gagarin felt before he took off, knowing that he might not come back alive? Would you risk your life for the sake of space exploration? Why or why not?

SOVIET SPACE CAPSULE–BETTMANN/CORBIS; ALL OTHER IMAGES–NASA

9   8   7   6

SURVIVING SPACE AND FAME

An article from *The Hindu*
By Olga Sobolevskaya, April 16, 2006

Yuri Gagarin's fame has not faded a bit since a huge rocket launched him into a near-Earth orbit on April 12, 1961. He became the first man to experience space weightlessness, not knowing for certain what effect it might have on his own life and health. He was the first to experience a speed of eight km per second [five mps], or more than 28,000 kilometers per hour [17,400 mph], something that heretofore was unthinkable. He was the first to be ... in a descent module engulfed in flames when entering the Earth's atmosphere. Yuri Gagarin was the first of all dwellers of the Earth to see it from space.

But he was not merely a man who was subjected to such an unforeseen experiment. Yuri Gagarin can by right be considered an expert who was on level with the scientists and engineers who prepared and carried out the flight of the spaceship *Vostok*. Not for a moment did he lose his self-control throughout the 108 minutes of his flight, in the course of which were critical moments, unpredictable and unexpected situations that nobody before him had ever experienced. ...

Presence of mind, restraint, courage, wisdom, quickness of thought, power of observation and sound knowledge — this is by far not everything that can be said of Yuri Gagarin. One could also mention his profound charm and modesty, for, after his flight, he was to face another serious test. He was the first and perhaps the only man to have experienced such worldwide fame in his life. ...

"It was the perfect choice," confirmed Gherman Titov. "Look at his biography. Yuri Gagarin is an ordinary man from Smolensk. ... He was a lad who made his dream come true all by himself ..."

---

engulfed: *enclosed*

Gagarin is on his way to the launch pad of Vostok I. *Behind him is his backup pilot, Gherman Titov.*

The Expert Says...

"Circling the Earth in the orbital spaceship, I marveled at the beauty of our planet. People of the world! Let us safeguard and enhance this beauty — not destroy it!

— Yuri Gagarin, Russian cosmonaut

Take Note

Putting the first human being into space broke new frontiers. It was a historic event and a milestone in space exploration. The *Vostok 1* mission opened up research in technology, medicine, and science. It is #1 on our list.

• Compare the impact of the first person in space aboard *Vostok 1* and the first astronaut on the moon [the *Apollo 11* mission at #2} on space exploration. Which mission is more important? Why?

1

5   4   3   2

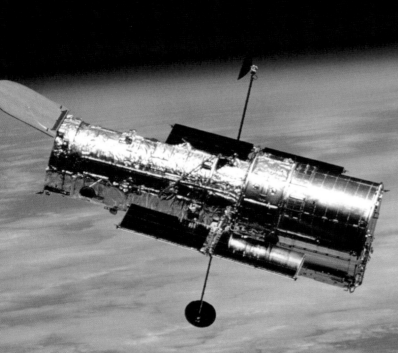

We Thought …

Here are the criteria we used in ranking the 10 greatest breakthroughs in space exploration.

The breakthrough:
- Influences space research
- Furthers space travel and discovery
- Creates friendly ties between countries
- Continues to open the door for experimentation
- Enables people to live in space
- Allows scientists to look closely at planets and the solar system
- Assists astronauts and cosmonauts to work in space
- Enables scientists to clearly see outside Earth's atmosphere
- Influences countries to improve their space missions

What Do You Think?

1. Do you agree with our ranking? If you don't, try ranking these breakthroughs yourself. Justify your ranking with data from your own research and reasoning. You may refer to our criteria, or you may want to draw up your own list of criteria.

2. Here are three other breakthroughs that we considered but in the end did not include in our top 10 list: communications satellites, *Gemini* space program, and *Skylab*.
   - Find out more about these breakthroughs. Do you think they should have made our list? Give reasons for your response.
   - Are there other breakthroughs in space exploration that you think should have made our list? Explain your choices.

Index